"HE SENT HIS WORD AND HEALED THEM, AND DELIVERED THEM FROM THEIR DESTRUCTIONS" (PSALM 107:20 NASB).

HE SENT HIS WORD AND
HEALED THEM

EVERY HEALING SCRIPTURE

Compiled by J.D. King

Christos Publishing

Printed in the United States of America
First Printing, 2018

ISBN 978-0-9992826-3-2

Christos Publishing
Lee's Summit, Missouri

Scripture quotations marked (NLT) are taken from the Holy Bible, New Living Translation, copyright © 1996, 2004, 2007, 2013, 2015 by Tyndale House Foundation. Used by permission of Tyndale House Publishers, Inc., Carol Stream, Illinois 60188. All rights reserved.

Scripture taken from the Holy Bible: International Standard Version (ISV) ®. Copyright © 1996-forever by The ISV Foundation. All rights reserved. Used by permission.

Scripture quotations marked (NIV) are taken from the Holy Bible, New International Version®, NIV®. Copyright © 1973, 1978, 1984, 2011 by Biblica, Inc.™ Used by permission of Zondervan. All rights reserved worldwide.

Scripture quotations marked (JUB) are taken from the Jubilee Bible, copyright © 2000, 2001, 2010, 2013 by Life Sentence Publishing, Inc. Used by permission of Life Sentence Publishing, Inc., Abbotsford, Wisconsin. All rights reserved.

Scripture quotations taken from the New American Standard Bible® (NASB), Copyright © 1960, 1962, 1963, 1968, 1971, 1972, 1973, 1975, 1977, 1995 by The Lockman Foundation. Used by permission.

Scripture taken from the New King James Version (NKJV) ®. Copyright © 1982 by Thomas Nelson. Used by permission. All rights reserved.

Quotations designated (NET©) are from the NET Bible® copyright ©1996-2017 by Biblical Studies Press, L.L.C. Used by permission. All rights reserved.

The Holy Bible, Berean Study Bible (BSB) Copyright ©2016 by Bible Hub. Used by Permission. All Rights Reserved Worldwide.

Weymouth New Testament (WNT), Copyright © 1903. Public Domain.

TO THE READER

The magnanimous heart of God is displayed in the Bible. Scripture declares that the Heavenly Father genuinely cares for His children. Although the darkness of affliction raises its ugly head, the Lord makes ample provision for healing. God is contending not only for the rejuvenation of the spirit and soul but also the body.

Throughout every section of scripture, divine healing is evidenced. The Old Testament parchments convey the life-giving prowess of our Creator. Physical deliverance is also conspicuous in the Gospels and other books of the New Testament. The Bible makes it abundantly clear that healing is rooted in God's advancing Kingdom.

Tragically, Christians often choose to live beneath heaven's provision. Due to skepticism and doubt, the works of God are marginalized. Tragically, many lower scripture to the level of their experience, rather than raise their experience to the level of scripture.

The Bible is the Word of God. It expresses inexplicable beauty and wonder. It has inexhaustible power. Rather than being constrained by the natural order, it supersedes it. Everything within the earthly realm is animated and sustained by the Word. Eventually, the visible will align with the invisible. Illness will be thwarted by the overcoming life of Jesus.

As one mediates on scripture, something extraordinary happens. The mind is renewed, and the heart is transformed. As the Word of God is courageously proclaimed, it counteracts darkness and disease. Confessing scripture brings health and life. The Apostle Paul asserted, "For with the heart one believes unto righteousness, and with the mouth confession is made unto saving health." (Romans 10:10 JUB). A confession is an act of faith that draws upon the abundant grace of God.

This book was compiled to encourage reflection, prayer, and biblical confession. Take time to meditate on these remarkable biblical passages. Underline some of the keywords and write brief observations in the margins. Declare healing scriptures over your loved ones and yourself. Intercede boldly. Engage God on multiple levels.

Jesus assures us that while the thief comes to steal, kill, and destroy, He has come that we might experience abundant life (John 10:10). Evil destroys, but God restores. In the midst of unspeakable affliction, God sent His word and released healing.

HE SENT HIS WORD AND
HEALED THEM

1. RESTORING FRUITFULNESS

"Then Abraham prayed to God, and God healed Abimelech, his wife, and his slave girls so they could have children again" (Genesis 20:17 NLT).

2. ENDING BARRENNESS

"Then God remembered Rachel; he listened to her and enabled her to conceive. She became pregnant and gave birth to a son and said, 'God has taken away my disgrace'" (Genesis 30:22-23 NIV).

3. ANTICIPATING GOD'S SAVING HEALTH

"I have waited for your saving health, O LORD" (Genesis 49:18 JUB).

4. THE BLOOD OF THE LAMB STOPS PLAGUES

"The blood will be a sign for you on the houses where you are, and when I see the blood, I will pass over you. No destructive plague will touch you when I strike Egypt" (Exodus 12:13 NIV).

5. THE SAVING HEALTH OF THE LORD

"Moses said unto the people, 'Fear not, stand still and see the saving health of the LORD, which he will bestow on you today; for the Egyptians whom you have seen today, you shall never see them again'" (Exodus 14:13 JUB).

6. THE LORD IS MY SAVING HEALTH

"The LORD is my strength and song, and He is my saving health; He is my God, and I will prepare him a habitation; my father's God, and I will exalt him" (Exodus 15:2 JUB).

7. THE GOD WHO WORKS WONDERS

"Who among the gods is like you, O LORD? Who is like you—majestic in holiness, awesome in glory, working wonders?" (Exodus 15:11 NIV).

8. YAHWEH RAPHA

"If you will listen carefully to the voice of the Lord your God and do what is right in his sight, obeying his commands and keeping all his decrees, then I will not make you suffer any of the diseases I sent on the Egyptians; for I am the Lord who heals you" (Exodus 15:26 NLT).

9. TAKING AWAY SICKNESS

"Worship the Lord your God, and his blessing will be on your food and water. I will take away sickness from among you" (Exodus 23:25 NIV).

10. PETITIONING GOD FOR HEALING

"As the cloud moved from above the Tabernacle, there stood Miriam, her skin as white as snow from leprosy. When Aaron saw what had happened to her, he cried out to Moses, 'Oh, my master! Please don't punish us for this sin we have so foolishly committed. Don't let her be like a stillborn baby, already decayed at birth.' So Moses cried out to the Lord, 'O God, I beg you, please heal her!'" (Numbers 12:10-13 NLT).

11. ATONEMENT STOPS THE PLAGUE

"Then Moses said to Aaron, 'Take your censer and put incense in it, along with fire from the altar, and hurry to the assembly to make atonement for them. Wrath has come out from the LORD; the plague has started.' So Aaron did as Moses said, and ran into the midst of the assembly. The plague had already started among the people, but Aaron offered the incense and made atonement for them. He stood between the living and the dead, and the plague stopped" (Numbers 16:46-48 NIV).

12. LOOK UPON THE SUFFERING SERVANT

"'We have sinned by speaking against the Lord and against you. Pray that the Lord will take away the snakes.' So Moses prayed for the people of Israel. Then the Lord told him, 'Make a replica of a poisonous snake and attach it to a pole. All who are bitten will live if they simply look at it!' So Moses made a snake out of bronze and attached it to a pole. Then anyone who was bitten by a snake could look at the bronze snake and be healed!" (Numbers 21:7-9 NIV).

13. GREAT POWER AND A SHOW OF FORCE

"You are to remember that you were a slave in the land of Egypt, but the LORD your God brought you out from there with great power and a show of force" (Deuteronomy 5:15a ISV).

14. PROTECTION FROM ALL SICKNESS

"The Lord will protect you from all sickness. He will not let you suffer from the terrible diseases you knew in Egypt" (Deuteronomy 7:15 NLT).

15. VIGOROUS AND STRONG

"Moses was 120 years old when he died. His eyesight wasn't impaired and he was still vigorous and strong" (Deuteronomy 34:7 ISV).

16. REVERSING INFERTILITY

"In those days a man named Manoah from the tribe of Dan lived in the town of Zorah. His wife was unable to become pregnant, and they had no children. The angel of the Lord appeared to Manoah's wife and said, 'Even though you have been unable to have children, you will soon become pregnant and give birth to a son' … When her son was born, she named him Samson. And the Lord blessed him as he grew up" (Judges 12:2-3, 24 NLT).

17. REMEMBERING TEAR-FILLED PLEAS

"Elkanah had two wives, Hannah and Peninnah. Peninnah had children, but Hannah did not … Peninnah would taunt Hannah and make fun of her because the Lord had kept her from having children. Year after year it was the same—Peninnah would taunt Hannah as they went to the Tabernacle. Each time, Hannah would be reduced to tears and would not even eat … The Lord remembered her plea, and in due time she gave birth to a son. She named him Samuel, for she said, 'I asked the Lord for him'" (1 Samuel 1:2, 7, 19-20 NLT).

18. HORN OF MY SAVING HEALTH

"God is my Strong One; in him will I trust: he is my shield and the horn of my saving health; my defense and my refuge; my savior, who shall save me from violence" (2 Samuel 22:3 JUB).

19. RESTORING A WITHERED HAND

"The king cried out to the man of God, 'Please ask the Lord your God to restore my hand again!' So the man of God prayed to the Lord, and the king's hand was restored and he could move it again" (1 Kings 13:6 NLT).

20. RESUSCITATION OF A DEAD CHILD

"Sometime later the woman's son became sick. He grew worse and worse, and finally he died. Then she said to Elijah, 'O man of God, what have you done to me? Have you come here to point out my sins and kill my son?' But Elijah replied, 'Give me your son.' And he took the child's body from her arms, carried him up the stairs to the room where he was staying, and laid the body on his bed. Then Elijah cried out to the Lord, 'O Lord my God, why have you brought tragedy to this widow who has opened her home to me, causing her son to die?' And he stretched himself out over the child three times and cried out to the Lord, 'O Lord my God, please let this child's life return to him.' The Lord heard Elijah's prayer, and the life of the child returned, and he revived!

Then Elijah brought him down from the upper room and gave him to his mother. 'Look!' he said. 'Your son is alive!' Then the woman told Elijah, 'Now I know for sure that you are a man of God, and that the Lord truly speaks through you'" (1 Kings 17:17-24 NLT).

21. REVERSING INFERTILITY

"Elisha said to his servant Gehazi, 'Tell the woman from Shunem I want to speak to her.' When she appeared, Elisha said to Gehazi, 'Tell her, 'We appreciate the kind concern you have shown us. What can we do for you? Can we put in a good word for you to the king or to the commander of the army?' 'No,' she replied, 'my family takes good care of me.' Later Elisha asked Gehazi, 'What can we do for her?' Gehazi replied, 'She doesn't have a son, and her husband is an old man.' 'Call her back again,' Elisha told him. When the woman returned, Elisha said to her as she stood in the doorway, 'Next year at this time you will be holding a son in your arms!' 'No, my lord!' she cried. 'O man of God, don't deceive me and get my hopes up like that.' But sure enough, the woman soon became pregnant. And at that time the following year she had a son, just as Elisha had said" (2 Kings 4:8-17 NLT).

22. LIFE FROM THE DEAD

"One day when her child was older, he went out to help his father, who was working with the harvesters. Suddenly he cried out, 'My head hurts! My head hurts!' His father said to one of the servants, 'Carry him home to his mother.' So the servant took him home, and his mother held him on her lap. But around noontime he died. She carried him up and laid him on the bed of the man of God, then shut the door and left him there. She sent a message to her husband: 'Send one of the servants and a donkey so that I can hurry to the man of God and come right back.' 'Why go today?' he asked. 'It is neither a new moon festival nor a Sabbath.' But she said, 'It will be all right.' So she saddled the donkey and said to the servant, 'Hurry! Don't slow down unless I tell you to.' As she approached the man of God at Mount Carmel, Elisha saw her in the distance. He said to Gehazi, 'Look, the woman from Shunem is coming. Run out to meet her and ask her, 'Is everything all right with you, your husband, and your child?' 'Yes,' the woman told Gehazi, 'everything is fine.' But when she came to the man of God at the mountain, she fell to the ground before him and caught hold of his feet. Gehazi began to push her away, but the man of God said, 'Leave her alone. She is deeply troubled, but the Lord has not told me what it is.' Then she said, 'Did I ask you for a son, my lord? And didn't I say, 'Don't deceive me and get my hopes up'? Then Elisha said to Gehazi, 'Get ready to travel; take my staff and go! Don't talk to anyone along the way. Go quickly and lay the staff on the child's face.' But the boy's mother said, 'As surely as the Lord lives and you yourself live, I won't go home unless you go with me.' So Elisha returned with her. Gehazi hurried on ahead and laid the staff on the child's face, but nothing happened. There was no sign of life. He returned to meet Elisha and told him, 'The child is still dead.' When Elisha arrived, the child was indeed dead, lying there on the prophet's bed. He went in alone and shut the door behind him and prayed to the Lord. Then he lay down on the child's body, placing his mouth on the child's mouth, his eyes on the child's eyes, and his hands on the child's hands. And as he stretched out on him, the child's body began to grow warm again! Elisha got up, walked back and forth across the room once, and then stretched himself out again on the child. This time the boy sneezed seven times and opened his eyes! Then Elisha summoned Gehazi. 'Call the child's mother!' he said. And when she came in, Elisha said, "Here, take your son!' She fell at his feet and bowed before him, overwhelmed with gratitude. Then she took her son in her arms and carried him downstairs" (2 Kings 4:18-37 NLT).

23. LEPROUS SKIN WASHED CLEAN

"Though Naaman was a mighty warrior, he suffered from leprosy. At this time Aramean raiders had invaded the land of Israel, and among their captives was a young girl who had been given to Naaman's wife as a maid. One day the girl said to her mistress, 'I wish my master would go to see the prophet in Samaria. He would heal him of his leprosy.' So Naaman told the king what the young girl from Israel had said. 'Go and visit the prophet,' the king of Aram told him. 'I will send a letter of introduction for you to take to the king of Israel.' So Naaman started out, carrying as gifts 750 pounds of silver, 150 pounds of gold, and ten sets of clothing. The letter to the king of Israel said: 'With this letter I present my servant Naaman. I want you to heal him of his leprosy.' When the king of Israel read the letter, he tore his clothes in dismay and said, 'Am I God, that I can give life and take it away? Why is this man asking me to heal someone with leprosy? I can see that he's just trying to pick a fight with me.' But when Elisha, the man of God, heard that the king of Israel had torn his clothes in dismay, he sent this message to him: 'Why are you so upset? Send Naaman to me, and he will learn that there is a true prophet here in Israel.' So Naaman went with his horses and chariots and waited at the door of Elisha's house. But Elisha sent a messenger out to him with this message: 'Go and wash yourself seven times in the Jordan River. Then your skin will be restored, and you will be healed of your leprosy.' But Naaman became angry and stalked away. 'I thought he would certainly come out to meet me!' he said, 'I expected him to wave his hand over the leprosy and call on the name of the Lord his God and heal me! Aren't the rivers of Damascus, the Abana and the Pharpar, better than any of the rivers of Israel? Why shouldn't I wash in them and be healed?' So Naaman turned and went away in a rage. But his officers tried to reason with him and said, 'Sir, if the prophet had told you to do something very difficult, wouldn't you have done it? So you should certainly obey him when he says simply, 'Go and wash and be cured!' So Naaman went down to the Jordan River and dipped himself seven times, as the man of God had instructed him. And his skin became as healthy as the skin of a young child, and he was healed!" (2 Kings 5:1-14 NLT).

24. POWER IN THE PROPHET'S BONES

"Once when some Israelites were burying a man, they spied a band of these raiders. So they hastily threw the corpse into the tomb of Elisha and fled. But as soon as the body touched Elisha's bones, the dead man revived and jumped to his feet!" (2 Kings 13:21 NLT).

25. RECOVERY OF KING HEZEKIAH

"About that time Hezekiah became deathly ill, and the prophet Isaiah son of Amoz went to visit him. He gave the king this message: 'This is what the Lord says: Set your affairs in order, for you are going to die. You will not recover from this illness.' When Hezekiah heard this, he turned his face to the wall and prayed to the Lord, 'Remember, O Lord, how I have always been faithful to you and have served you single-mindedly, always doing what pleases you.' Then he broke down and wept bitterly. But before Isaiah had left the middle courtyard, this message came to him from the Lord: 'Go back to Hezekiah, the leader of my people. Tell him, 'This is what the Lord, the God of your ancestor David, says: I have heard your prayer and seen your tears. I will heal you, and three days from now you will get out of bed and go to the Temple of the Lord. I will add fifteen years to your life, and I will rescue you and this city from the king of Assyria. I will defend this city for my own honor and for the sake of my servant David.' Then Isaiah said, 'Make an ointment from figs.' So Hezekiah's servants spread the ointment over the boil, and Hezekiah recovered!" (2 Kings 20:1-7 NLT).

26. THE LORD STRENGTHENS

"The eyes of the LORD range throughout the earth to strengthen those whose hearts are fully committed to him" (2 Chronicles 16:9a NIV).

27. THE LORD HEARS AND DELIVERS

"If evil comes upon us, such as war as punishment, disease, or famine and we stand in your presence in this Temple (because your Name is in this Temple) and cry out to you in our distress, then you will hear and deliver" (2 Chronicles 20:9 ISV).

28. THE LORD LISTENED AND HEALED

"Hezekiah said, 'May the Lord, who is good, pardon those who decide to follow the Lord, the God of their ancestors, even though they are not properly cleansed for the ceremony.' And the Lord listened to Hezekiah's prayer and healed the people" (2 Chronicles 30:19-20 NLT).

29. A MIRACULOUS SIGN

"About that time Hezekiah became deathly ill. He prayed to the Lord, who healed him and gave him a miraculous sign" (2 Chronicles 32:24 NLT).

30. THE JOY OF THE LORD BRINGS STRENGTH

"Don't be dejected and sad, for the joy of the LORD is your strength!" (Nehemiah 8:10 NLT).

31. RECOVER THE STRENGTH OF YOUTH

"Let his flesh be rejuvenated as he was in his youth! Let him recover the strength of his youth" (Job 33:25 ISV).

32. ENJOYING THE LIGHT OF LIFE

"God rescued me from the grave and now my life is filled with light. Yes, God does these things again and again for people. He rescues them from the grave so they may enjoy the light of life" (Job 33:29-30 NLT).

33. THE LORD DOES NOT AFFLICT

"The Almighty … is excellent in power, in judgment, and abundant justice. He does not afflict" (Job 37:23 NKJV).

34. HEALING FOR BONES IN AGONY

"Have compassion on me, Lord, for I am weak. Heal me, Lord, for my bones are in agony" (Psalm 6:2 NLT).

35. REJOICE IN GOD'S DELIVERANCE

"Look at me! Answer me, Lord, my God! Give light to my eyes! Otherwise, I will sleep in death; Otherwise, my enemy will say, 'I have overcome him;' Otherwise, my persecutor will rejoice when I am shaken. As for me, I have trusted in your gracious love, my heart will rejoice in your deliverance" (Psalm 13:3-5 ISV).

36. RESCUING THE AFFLICTED

"You rescue an afflicted people, but You humble those with haughty eyes" (Psalm 18:27 NASB).

37. GOD HEARS THE AFFLICTED

"For he does not despise nor detest the afflicted person; he does not hide his face from him, but he hears him when he cries out to him" (Psalm 22:24 ISV).

38. HEALING FOR THE AFFLICTED

"Turn to me and be gracious to me, for I am lonely and afflicted" (Psalm 25:16 NIV).

39. THE GOODNESS OF THE LORD

"I remain confident of this: I will see the goodness of the LORD in the land of the living" (Psalm 27:13 NIV).

40. CRY TO GOD FOR HELP

"O Lord my God, I cried to You for help, and You healed me" (Psalm 30:2 NASB).

41. THE HIDING PLACE

"For you are my hiding place; you protect me from trouble. You surround me with songs of victory" (Psalm 32:7 NLT).

42. DELIVERED FROM ALL AFFLICTIONS

"Many are the afflictions of the righteous, but the LORD delivers him out of them all" (Psalm 34:19 NASB).

43. GOD DELIGHTS IN THE WELL-BEING OF HIS SERVANTS

"May those who delight in my vindication shout for joy and gladness; may they always say, 'The Lord be exalted, who delights in the well-being of his servant'" (Psalm 35:27 NIV).

44. COME QUICKLY

"Do not abandon me, O LORD. Do not stand at a distance, my God. Come quickly to help me, O Lord my savior" (Psalm 38:21-22 NLT).

45. RESTORED FROM A BED OF ILLNESS

"Blessed is he who has regard for the weak; the Lord delivers him in times of trouble. The Lord will protect him and preserve his life; he will bless him in the land and not surrender him to the desire of his foes. The Lord will sustain him on his sickbed and restore him from his bed of illness I said, 'O Lord, have mercy on me; heal me, for I have sinned against you'" (Psalm 41:1-4 NIV).

46. THE SAVING HEALTH OF MY COUNTENANCE

"Why art thou cast down, O my soul? and why art thou disquieted within me? Wait thou for God, for I shall yet praise him, who is the saving health of my countenance and my God" (Psalm 42:11 JUB).

47. WHY ARE YOU DOWNCAST O MY SOUL?

"Why are you cast down, O my soul? and why are you disquieted within me? Wait for God, for I shall yet praise him, who is the saving health of my countenance and my God" (Psalm 43:5 JUB).

48. CAUSE YOUR FACE TO SHINE UPON US

"God be merciful to us and bless us and cause Your face to shine upon us. Selah. That Your way may be known upon the earth, Your saving health among all the Gentiles" (Psalm 67:1-2 JUB).

49. THE LORD HEARS THE CRIES OF THE NEEDY

"I am suffering and in pain. Rescue me, O God, by your saving power. Then I will praise God's name with singing, and I will honor him with thanksgiving. For this will please the Lord more than sacrificing cattle, more than presenting a bull with its horns and hooves. The humble will see their God at work and be glad. Let all who seek God's help be encouraged. For the Lord hears the cries of the needy; he does not despise his imprisoned people" (Psalm 69:29-33 NLT).

50. I DECLARE YOUR MARVELOUS DEEDS

"Since my youth, God, you have taught me, and to this day I declare your marvelous deeds. Even when I am old and gray, do not forsake me, my God, I declare your power to the next generation, your mighty acts to all who are to come. Your righteousness, God, reaches to the heavens, you who have done great things. Who is like you, God? Though you have made me see troubles, many and bitter, you will restore my life again; from the depths of the earth you will again bring me up. You will increase my honor and comfort me once more" (Psalm 71:17-21 NIV).

51. THE GOD WHO PERFORMS MIRACLES

"Will the Lord reject forever? Will he never show his favor again? Has his unfailing love vanished forever? Has His promise failed for all time? Has God forgotten to be merciful? Has he in anger withheld his compassion? Then I thought, 'To this will I appeal: the years of the right hand of the Most High.' I will remember the deeds of the LORD; yes, I will remember your miracles of long ago. I will meditate on all your works and consider all your mighty deeds. Your ways, O God, are holy. What God is so great as our God? You are the God who performs miracles; you display your power among the peoples" (Psalm 77:7-14 NIV).

52. HEAL ME—FOR ONLY THE LIVING PRAISE YOU

"Do you show your wonders to the dead? Do those who are dead rise up and praise you? Is your love declared in the grave, your faithfulness in destruction? Are your wonders known in the place of darkness, or your righteous deeds in the land of oblivion?" (Psalm 88:10-12 NIV).

53. PLAGUE WILL NOT COME NEAR YOUR HOME

"No evil befall you, neither shall any plague come near your dwelling. . . With long life will I satisfy him, and show him my salvation" (Psalm 91:10, 16 NKJV).

54. FORGIVING SIN AND HEALING DISEASE

"Let all that I am praise the Lord; with my whole heart, I will praise his holy name. Let all that I am praise the Lord; may I never forget the good things he does for me. He forgives all my sins and heals all my diseases. He redeems me from death and crowns me with love and tender mercies" (Psalm 103:1-4 NLT).

55. NO FEEBLE AMONG ISRAEL

"God also brought the children of Israel out with silver and gold, and there was none feeble among His tribes" (Psalm 105:37 NKJV).

56. GOD SENT HIS WORD AND HEALED THEM

"He sent out his word and healed them, snatching them from the door of death" (Psalm 107:20 NLT).

57. MAY I LIVE—ONLY THE LIVING PRAISE THE LORD

"It is not the dead who praise the Lord, those who go down to silence; it is we who extol the Lord, both now and forevermore" (Psalm 115:17-18 NIV).

58. THE LORD HAS BEEN GOOD TO ME

"I love the Lord because he hears my voice and my prayer for mercy. Because he bends down to listen, I will pray as long as I have breath! Death wrapped its ropes around me; the terrors of the grave overtook me. I saw only trouble and sorrow. Then I called on the name of the Lord: 'Please, Lord, save me!' How kind the Lord is! How good he is! So merciful, this God of ours! The Lord protects those of childlike faith; I was facing death, and he saved me. Let my soul be at rest again, for the Lord has been good to me. He has saved me from death, my eyes from tears, my feet from stumbling. And so I walk in the Lord's presence as I live here on earth!" (Psalm 116:1-9 NLT).

59. I SHALL NOT DIE, BUT LIVE

"I shall not die, but live, and declare the works of the LORD" (Psalm 118:17 NKJV).

60. REVIVE ME

"I am exceedingly afflicted; Revive me, O LORD, according to Your word" (Psalm 119:107 NASB).

61. COMFORT IN MY AFFLICTION

"Remember your promise to me; it is my only hope. This is my comfort in my affliction, for Your word has given me life" (Psalm 119:49-50 NLT).

62. THE LORD IS GOOD TO EVERYONE

"The LORD is merciful and compassionate, slow to get angry and filled with unfailing love. The LORD is good to everyone. He showers compassion on all his creation" (Psalm 145:8-9 NLT).

63. GOD OPENS THE EYES OF THE BLIND

"The Lord opens the eyes of the blind. The Lord lifts up those who are weighed down" (Psalm 146:8 NLT).

64. GOD HEALS THE BROKENHEARTED

"He heals the brokenhearted and binds up their wounds" (Psalm 147:3 NIV).

65. UNTROUBLED BY FEAR OF HARM

"All who listen to me will live in peace, untroubled by fear of harm" (Proverbs 1:33 NLT).

66. HEALING FOR YOUR BODY AND STRENGTH FOR YOUR BONES

"Don't be impressed with your own wisdom. Instead, fear the Lord and turn away from evil. Then you will have healing for your body and strength for your bones" (Proverbs 3:7-8 NLT).

67. HEALING WORDS TO THE BODY

"My child, pay attention to what I say. Listen carefully to my words. Don't lose sight of them. Let them penetrate deep into your heart, for they bring life to those who find them, and healing to their whole body" (Proverbs 4:20-22 NLT).

68. WISDOM BRINGS LIFE

"Whoever finds wisdom finds life and receives favor from the Lord. But those who miss me injure themselves. All who hate me love death" (Proverbs 8:35-36 NLT).

69. GODLY HONOR LENGTHENS LIFE

"Fear of the LORD lengthens one's life, but the years of the wicked are cut short" (Proverbs 10:27 NLT).

70. THE TONGUE OF THE WISE BRINGS HEALING

"Reckless words pierce like a sword, but the tongue of the wise brings healing" (Proverbs 12:18 NIV).

71. HOPELESSNESS INSTILLS SICKNESS

"Hope deferred makes the heart sick, but a longing fulfilled is a tree of life" (Proverbs 13:12 NIV).

72. WISDOM IS A LIFE-GIVING FOUNTAIN

"Instruction from the wise is like a life-giving fountain, to turn a person from deadly snares" (Proverbs 13:14 NET).

73. AN HONORABLE MESSENGER BRINGS HEALING

"A trustworthy envoy brings healing" (Proverbs 13:17b NIV).

74. A PEACEFUL HEART BRINGS HEALTH

"A peaceful heart leads to a healthy body; jealousy is like cancer in the bones" (Proverbs 14:30 NLT).

75. A HEALING TONGUE IS A TREE OF LIFE

"The tongue that heals is a tree of life, but a devious tongue breaks the spirit" (Proverbs 15:4 NLT).

76. GOOD NEWS GIVES HEALTH TO THE BONES

"Light in a messenger's eyes brings joy to the heart, and good news gives health to the bones" (Proverbs 15:30 NIV).

77. INSIGHT IS A FOUNTAIN OF LIFE

"Insight is a fountain of life for its possessor" (Proverbs 16:22 HSB).

78. PLEASANT WORDS ARE HEALING FOR THE BODY

"Pleasant words are honey from a honeycomb—sweet to the soul and healing for the body" (Proverbs 16:24 ISV).

79. A JOYFUL HEART IS GOOD MEDICINE

"A joyful heart is good medicine, but a broken spirit dries up the bones" (Proverbs 17:22 ISV).

80. DEATH AND LIFE ARE IN THE POWER OF THE TONGUE

"Death and life are in the power of the tongue, and those who love it will eat its fruit" (Proverbs 18:21 HSBC).

81. THE PURSUIT OF RIGHTEOUSNESS BRINGS LIFE

"Whoever pursues righteousness and love finds life, prosperity, and honor" (Proverbs 21:21 NIV).

82. DON'T TOIL FOR THE WIND

"What is the advantage to him who toils for the wind? Throughout his life he also eats in darkness with great vexation, sickness and anger" (Ecclesiastes 5:16-17 NASB).

83. THE YOKE IS DESTROYED BECAUSE OF THE ANOINTING

"It shall come to pass in that day that his burden will be taken away from your shoulder, and his yoke from your neck, and the yoke will be destroyed because of the anointing oil" (Isaiah 10:27 NKJV).

84. THE LORD HEARS PLEAS AND HE HEALS

"The Egyptians will turn to the Lord, and he will listen to their pleas and heal them" (Isaiah 19:22b NLT).

85. FAITHFUL ONES ARE KEPT COMPLETELY SAFE

"You keep completely safe the people who maintain their faith, for they trust in you" (Isaiah 26:3 NET).

86. THE DEAF HEAR AND THE BLIND SEE

"In that day, the deaf will hear the words of the scroll, and out of gloom and darkness the eyes of the blind will see" (Isaiah 29:18 NIV).

87. THE MOON AND SUN WILL SHINE BRIGHTER

"The moon will be as bright as the sun, and the sun will be seven times brighter--like the light of seven days in one! So it will be when the LORD begins to heal his people" (Isaiah 30:26a NLT).

88. LIKE STREAMS OF WATER IN A DRY PLACE

"Behold, a king will reign in righteousness, and princes will rule in justice. Each will be like a hiding place from the wind, a shelter from the storm, like streams of water in a dry place, like the shade of a great rock in a weary land. Then the eyes of those who see will not be closed, and the ears of those who hear will give attention. The heart of the hasty will understand and know, and the tongue of the stammerers will hasten to speak distinctly" (Isaiah 32:1-4 ESV).

89. A SURE FOUNDATION

"In that day, the Lord will be your sure foundation, providing a rich store of salvation, wisdom, and knowledge. The fear of the Lord will be your treasure … The people of Israel will no longer say, 'We are sick and helpless'" (Isaiah 33:5-6, 24a NLT).

90. WHEN HE COMES

"When he comes, he will open the eyes of the blind and unplug the ears of the deaf. The lame will leap like a deer, and those who cannot speak will sing for joy!" (Isaiah 35:5-6a NLT).

91. I WILL ADD YEARS TO YOUR LIFE

"Hezekiah became deathly ill, and the prophet Isaiah son of Amoz went to visit him. He gave the king this message: 'This is what the Lord says: 'Set your affairs in order, for you are going to die. You will not recover from this illness.' When Hezekiah heard this, he turned his face to the wall and prayed to the Lord, 'Remember, O Lord, how I have always been faithful to you and have served you single-mindedly, always doing what pleases you.' Then he broke down and wept bitterly. Then this message came to Isaiah from the Lord: 'Go back to Hezekiah and tell him, 'This is what the Lord, the God of your ancestor David, says: I have heard your prayer and seen your tears. I will add fifteen years to your life, and I will rescue you and this city from the king of Assyria. Yes, I will defend this city.'

And this is the sign from the Lord to prove that he will do as he promised: I will cause the sun's shadow to move ten steps backward on the sundial of Ahaz!' So the shadow on the sundial moved backward ten steps" (Isaiah 38:1-8 NLT).

92. YOU RESTORED ME TO HEALTH

"Lord, by such things people live; and my spirit finds life in them too. You restored me to health and let me live" (Isaiah 38:16 NIV).

93. THOSE SICK INTO DEATH CANNOT PRAISE YOU

"For the grave cannot praise you, death cannot sing your praise; those who go down to the pit cannot hope for your faithfulness. The living, the living—they praise you, as I am doing today; fathers tell their children about your faithfulness" (Isaiah 38:18-19 NIV).

94. GOD INCREASES STRENGTH

"He gives power to the faint, and to him who has no might he increases strength" (Isaiah 40:29 ESV).

95. NEW STRENGTH

"Those who trust in the LORD will find new strength. They will soar high on wings like eagles. They will run and not grow weary. They will walk and not faint" (Isaiah 40:31 NLT).

96. DO NOT FEAR, GOD IS WITH YOU

"Do not fear, for I am with you; do not be dismayed, for I am your God. I will strengthen you and help you; I will uphold you with my righteous right hand" (Isaiah 41:10 NIV).

97. EVEN IN YOUR GRAYING YEARS, I WILL BEAR YOU

"Even to your old age I will be the same, and even to your graying years I will bear you! I have done it, and I will carry you; and I will bear you and I will deliver you" (Isaiah 46:4 NASB).

98. BY HIS WOUNDS WE ARE HEALED

"Surely he took up our infirmities and carried our sorrows, yet we considered him stricken by God, smitten by him, and afflicted. But he was pierced for our transgressions, he was crushed for our iniquities; the punishment that brought us peace was upon him, and by his wounds we are healed" (Isaiah 53:4-5 NKJV).

99. I WILL HEAL THEM ANYWAY

"'I have seen what they do, but I will heal them anyway! I will lead them. I will comfort those who mourn, bringing words of praise to their lips. May they have abundant peace, both near and far,' says the Lord, who heals them" (Isaiah 57:18-19 NLT).

100. WOUNDS WILL QUICKLY HEAL

"Your salvation will come like the dawn, and your wounds will quickly heal. Your godliness will lead you forward, and the glory of the Lord will protect you from behind" (Isaiah 58:8 NLT).

101. THE BLIND WILL SEE

"The Spirit of the Sovereign Lord is upon me, for the Lord has anointed me to bring good news to the poor. He has sent me to comfort the brokenhearted and to proclaim that captives will be released and the blind will see" (Isaiah 61:1 NLT).

102. IS THERE NO HEALING FOR GOD'S PEOPLE?

"I hurt with the hurt of my people. I mourn and am overcome with grief. Is there no medicine in Gilead? Is there no physician there? Why is there no healing for the wounds of my people?" (Jeremiah 8:21-22 NLT).

103. IF YOU RETURN TO GOD, HE WILL RESTORE YOU

'If you return to me, I will restore you so you can continue to serve me" (Jeremiah 15:19 NLT).

104. IF GOD HEALS ME, I WILL BE TRULY HEALED

"O Lord, if you heal me, I will be truly healed; if you save me, I will be truly saved. My praises are for you alone!" (Jeremiah 17:14 NLT).

105. PLANS TO GIVE YOU HOPE

"'For I know the plans I have for you,' declares the LORD, 'plans to prosper you and not to harm you, plans to give you hope and a future'" (Jeremiah 29:11 NIV).

106. I WILL GIVE YOU BACK YOUR HEALTH

"'All who devour you will be devoured, and all your enemies will be sent into exile. All who plunder you will be plundered, and all who attack you will be attacked. I will give you back your health and heal your wounds,' says the Lord" (Jeremiah 30:16-17a NLT).

107. I WILL HEAL MY PEOPLE

"Nevertheless, I will bring health and healing to it; I will heal my people and will let them enjoy abundant peace and security" (Jeremiah 33:6 NIV).

108. LIVE

"On the day you were born, no one cared about you. Your umbilical cord was not cut, and you were never washed, rubbed with salt, and wrapped in cloth. No one had the slightest interest in you; no one pitied you or cared for you. On the day you were born, you were unwanted, dumped in a field and left to die. But I came by and saw you there, helplessly kicking about in your own blood. As you lay there, I said, 'Live!' And I helped you to thrive like a plant in the field. You grew up and became a beautiful jewel" (Ezekiel 16:4-7a NLT).

109. I WILL STRENGTHEN THE SICK

"I will seek the lost, bring back the scattered, bind up the broken and strengthen the sick" (Ezekiel 34:16 NASB).

110. MY SPIRIT WILL BE PLACED IN YOU AND YOU WILL LIVE

"I'm going to place my Spirit in you all, and you will live. I'll place you all into your land, and you'll learn that I, the LORD, have been speaking and doing this" (Ezekiel 37:14 ISV).

111. LEAVES OF HEALING

"This water flows toward the eastern region and goes down into the Arabah, where it enters the Sea. When it empties into the Sea, the water there becomes fresh. Swarms of living creatures will live wherever the river flows ... Fruit trees of all kinds will grow on both banks of the river. Their leaves will not wither, nor will their fruit fail. Every month they will bear, because the water from the sanctuary flows to them. Their fruit will serve for food and their leaves for healing" (Ezekiel 47:8, 12 NIV).

112. THEY DID NOT KNOW THAT I HEALED THEM

"It is I who taught Ephraim to walk, I took them in My arms; But they did not know that I healed them" (Hosea 11:3 ESV).

113. SEEK ME AND LIVE

"For this is what the LORD says to the house of Israel: 'Seek me and live'" (Amos 5:4 ISV).

114. DON'T FORFEIT THE MERCY

"Those who regard worthless things forfeit the mercy that could be theirs. But as for me, with a voice of thanksgiving I will sacrifice to you; what I have vowed I will pay. Deliverance is the LORD's!" (Jonah 2:8-9 NET).

115. THE LAME WILL BE GATHERED

"'In that day,' declares the LORD, 'I will gather the lame; I will assemble the exiles and those I have brought to grief'" (Micah 4:6 NIV).

116. RESCUE THE LAME

"At that time I will deal with all who oppressed you. I will rescue the lame; I will gather the exiles. I will give them praise and honor in every land where they have suffered shame" (Zephaniah 3:19 NIV).

117. HEALING IN HIS WINGS

"For you who fear my name, the sun of righteousness will rise with healing in his wings. And you will go free, leaping with joy like calves let out to pasture" (Malachi 4:2 ESV).

118. "JESUS," MEANS "GOD HEALS"

"She will give birth to a son, and you are to give him the name Jesus [God heals], because he will save his people from their sins" (Matthew 1:21 NIV).

119. HEALING EVERY DISEASE

"Then he went throughout Galilee, teaching in their synagogues, proclaiming the gospel of the kingdom, and healing every disease and every illness among the people. His fame spread throughout Syria, and people brought to him everyone who was sick—those afflicted with various diseases and pains, the demon-possessed, the epileptics, and the paralyzed—and he healed them" (Matthew 4:23-24 ISV).

120. EARS OPENED AND TONGUE LOOSED

"After he took him aside, away from the crowd, Jesus put his fingers into the man's ears. Then he spit and touched the man's tongue. He looked up to heaven and with a deep sigh said to him, 'Ephphatha!' (which means 'Be opened!'). At this, the man's ears were opened, his tongue was loosened and he began to speak plainly" (Matthew 7:33-35 NIV).

121. I AM WILLING TO HEAL

"A man with leprosy came and knelt before him and said, 'Lord, if you are willing, you can make me clean.' Jesus reached out his hand and touched the man. 'I am willing,' he said. 'Be clean!' Immediately he was cleansed of his leprosy" (Matthew 8:2-4 NIV).

122. HEALING AN OFFICER'S SERVANT

"When Jesus returned to Capernaum, a Roman officer came and pleaded with him, 'Lord, my young servant lies in bed, paralyzed and in terrible pain.' Jesus said, 'I will come and heal him.' But the officer said, 'Lord, I am not worthy to have you come into my home. Just say the word from where you are, and my servant will be healed. I know this because I am under the authority of my superior officers, and I have authority over my soldiers. I only need to say, 'Go,' and they go, or 'Come,' and they come. And if I say to my slaves, 'Do this,' they do it.' When Jesus heard this, he was amazed. Turning to those who were following him, he said, 'I tell you the truth, I haven't seen faith like this in all Israel! And I tell you this, that many Gentiles will come from all over the world—from east and west—and sit down with Abraham, Isaac, and Jacob at the feast in the Kingdom of Heaven. But many Israelites—those for whom the Kingdom was prepared—will be thrown into outer darkness, where there will be weeping and gnashing of teeth.' Then Jesus said to the Roman officer, 'Go back home. Because you believed, it has happened.' And the young servant was healed that same hour" (Matthew 8:5-13 NLT).

123. PETER'S MOTHER-IN-LAW RESTORED

"When Jesus arrived at Peter's house, Peter's mother-in-law was sick in bed with a high fever. But when Jesus touched her hand, the fever left her. Then she got up and prepared a meal for him. That evening many demon-possessed people were brought to Jesus. He cast out the evil spirits with a simple command, and he healed all the sick. This fulfilled the word of the Lord through the prophet Isaiah, who said, 'He took our sicknesses and removed our diseases'" (Matthew 8:14-17 NLT).

124. BREAKTHROUGH FOR A PARALYZED MAN

"Some men brought to him a paralyzed man, lying on a mat. When Jesus saw their faith, he said to the man, 'Take heart, son; your sins are forgiven.' Which is easier: to say, 'Your sins are forgiven,' or to say, 'Get up and walk'? But I want you to know that the Son of Man has authority on earth to forgive sins.' So he said to the paralyzed man, 'Get up, take your mat and go home.' Then the man got up and went home. When the crowd saw this, they were filled with awe; and they praised God, who had given such authority to man" (Matthew 9:2-8 NIV).

125. AN AFFLICTED WOMAN MADE WHOLE

"Just then a woman who had suffered for twelve years with constant bleeding came up behind him. She touched the fringe of his robe, for she thought, 'If I can just touch his robe, I will be healed.' Jesus turned around, and when he saw her he said, 'Daughter, be encouraged! Your faith has made you well.' And the woman was healed at that moment" (Matthew 9:20-22 NLT).

126. A SYNAGOGUE LEADER'S DAUGHTER IS RESUSCITATED

"When Jesus entered the synagogue leader's house and saw the noisy crowd and people playing pipes, he said, 'Go away. The girl is not dead but asleep.' But they laughed at him. After the crowd had been put outside, he went in and took the girl by the hand, and she got up" (Matthew 9:23-25 NIV).

127. EVERY KIND OF DISEASE HEALED BY JESUS

"Jesus traveled through all the towns and villages of that area, teaching in the synagogues and announcing the Good News about the Kingdom. And He healed every kind of disease and illness" (Matthew 9:35 NLT).

128. HEAL THE SICK!

"Jesus called his twelve disciples together and gave them authority to cast out evil spirits and to heal every kind of disease and illness ... Heal the sick, raise the dead, cure those with leprosy, and cast out demons. Give as freely as you have received!" (Matthew 10:1, 8 NLT).

129. ISAIAH 35 FULFILLED

"John the Baptist, who was in prison, heard about all the things the Messiah was doing. So he sent his disciples to ask Jesus, 'Are you the Messiah we've been expecting, or should we keep looking for someone else?' Jesus told them, 'Go back to John and tell him what you have heard and seen— the blind see, the lame walk, those with leprosy are cured, the deaf hear, the dead are raised to life, and the Good News is being preached to the poor'" (Matthew 11:2-5 NLT).

130. DOING GOOD ON THE SABBATH

"Then Jesus went over to their synagogue, where he noticed a man with a deformed hand. The Pharisees asked Jesus, 'Does the law permit a person to work by healing on the Sabbath?' (They were hoping he would say yes, so they could bring charges against him.) And he answered, 'If you had a sheep that fell into a well on the Sabbath, wouldn't you work to pull it out? Of course you would. And how much more valuable is a person than a sheep! Yes, the law permits a person to do good on the Sabbath.' Then he said to the man, 'Hold out your hand.' So the man held out his hand, and it was restored, just like the other one!" (Matthew 12:9-13 NLT).

131. JESUS HEALED ALL THE SICK

"Jesus left that area, and many people followed him. He healed all the sick among them" (Matthew 12:15 NKJV).

132. UNBELIEF HINDERS

"He returned to Nazareth, his hometown. When he taught there in the synagogue, everyone was amazed and said, 'Where does he get this wisdom and the power to do miracles?' Then they scoffed, 'He's just the carpenter's son, and we know Mary, his mother, and his brothers—James, Joseph, Simon, and Judas. All his sisters live right here among us. Where did he learn all these things?' And they were deeply offended and refused to believe in him. Then Jesus told them, 'A prophet is honored everywhere except in his own hometown and among his own family.' And so he did only a few miracles there because of their unbelief" (Matthew 13:54-58 NLT).

133. HEALING FLOWS OUT OF COMPASSION

"Jesus saw the huge crowd as he stepped from the boat, and he had compassion on them and healed their sick" (Matthew 14:14 NLT).

134. ALL WHO TOUCHED JESUS WERE HEALED

"After they had crossed the lake, they landed at Gennesaret. When the people recognized Jesus, the news of his arrival spread quickly throughout the whole area, and soon people were bringing all their sick to be healed. They begged him to let the sick touch at least the fringe of his robe, and all who touched him were healed" (Matthew 14:34-36 NLT).

135. HEALING IS THE CHILDREN'S BREAD

"A Gentile woman who lived there came to him, pleading, 'Have mercy on me, O Lord, Son of David! For my daughter is possessed by a demon that torments her severely.' But Jesus gave her no reply, not even a word. Then his disciples urged him to send her away. 'Tell her to go away,' they said. 'She is bothering us with all her begging.' Then Jesus said to the woman, 'I was sent only to help God's lost sheep—the people of Israel.' But she came and worshiped him, pleading again, 'Lord, help me!' Jesus responded, 'It isn't right to take food from the children and throw it to the dogs.' She replied, 'That's true, Lord, but even dogs are allowed to eat the scraps that fall beneath their masters' table.' 'Dear woman,' Jesus said to her, 'your faith is great. Your request is granted.' And her daughter was instantly healed" (Matthew 15:22-29 NLT).

136. AND HE HEALED THEM ALL

"Jesus returned to the Sea of Galilee and climbed a hill and sat down. A vast crowd brought to him people who were lame, blind, crippled, those who couldn't speak, and many others. They laid them before Jesus, and he healed them all. The crowd was amazed! Those who hadn't been able to speak were talking, the crippled were made well, the lame were walking, and the blind could see again! And they praised the God of Israel" (Matthew 15:29-31 NLT).

137. AN AFFLICTED BOY HEALED

"At the foot of the mountain, a large crowd was waiting for them. A man came and knelt before Jesus and said, 'Lord, have mercy on my son. He has seizures and suffers terribly. He often falls into the fire or into the water. So I brought him to your disciples, but they couldn't heal him.' Jesus said, 'You faithless and corrupt people! How long must I be with you? How long must I put up with you? Bring the boy here to me.' Then Jesus rebuked the demon in the boy, and it left him. From that moment the boy was well" (Matthew 17:14-18 NLT).

138. JESUS HEALED THE CROWDS

"When Jesus had finished saying these things, he left Galilee and went down to the region of Judea east of the Jordan River. Large crowds followed him there, and he healed their sick" (Matthew 19:1-2 NLT).

139. WITH GOD ALL THINGS ARE POSSIBLE

"Jesus looked at them and said, 'With man this is impossible, but with God all things are possible'" (Matthew 19:26 NIV).

140. BLIND MEN RESTORED TO SIGHT

"Two blind men were sitting beside the road. When they heard that Jesus was coming that way, they began shouting, 'Lord, Son of David, have mercy on us!' 'Be quiet!' the crowd yelled at them. But they only shouted louder, 'Lord, Son of David, have mercy on us!' When Jesus heard them, he stopped and called, 'What do you want me to do for you?' 'Lord,' they said, 'We want to see!' Jesus felt sorry for them and touched their eyes. Instantly they could see! Then they followed him" (Matthew 20:30-34 NLT).

141. HEALING THE LAME AND BLIND

"The blind and the lame came to him at the temple, and he healed them" (Matthew 21:14 NIV).

142. THE SICK WERE BROUGHT TO JESUS

"That evening after sunset, many sick and demon-possessed people were brought to Jesus. The whole town gathered at the door to watch. So Jesus healed many people who were sick with various diseases, and he cast out many demons" (Mark 1:32-34 NLT).

143. A MAN WITH LEPROSY HEALED

"A man with leprosy came and knelt in front of Jesus, begging to be healed. 'If you are willing, you can heal me and make me clean,' he said. Moved with compassion, Jesus reached out and touched him. 'I am willing,' he said. 'Be healed!' Instantly the leprosy disappeared, and the man was healed" (Mark 1:40-42 NLT).

144. JESUS HEALS A PARALYTIC

"Some men came, bringing to him a paralytic, carried by four of them. Since they could not get him to Jesus because of the crowd, they made an opening in the roof above Jesus and, after digging through it, lowered the mat the paralyzed man was lying on. When Jesus saw their faith, he said to the paralytic, 'Son, your sins are forgiven.' Now some teachers of the law were sitting there, thinking to themselves, 'Why does this fellow talk like that? He's blaspheming! Who can forgive sins but God alone?' Immediately Jesus knew in his spirit that this was what they were thinking in their hearts, and he said to them, 'Why are you thinking these things? Which is easier: to say to the paralytic, 'Your sins are forgiven,' or to say, 'Get up, take your mat and walk'? But that you may know that the Son of Man has authority on earth to forgive sins....' He said to the paralytic, 'I tell you, get up, take your mat and go home'" (Mark 2:3-11 NIV).

145. THE HEALING OF A HAND

"Jesus went into the synagogue again and noticed a man with a deformed hand. Since it was the Sabbath, Jesus' enemies watched him closely. If he healed the man's hand, they planned to accuse him of working on the Sabbath. Jesus said to the man with the deformed hand, 'Come and stand in front of everyone.' Then he turned to his critics and asked, 'Does the law permit good deeds on the Sabbath, or is it a day for doing evil? Is this a day to save life or to destroy it?' But they wouldn't answer him. He looked around at them angrily and was deeply saddened by their hard hearts. Then he said to the man, 'Hold out your hand.' So the man held out his hand, and it was restored!" (Mark 3:1-5 NLT).

146. SICK PEOPLE TOUCH JESUS

"The news about Jesus' miracles had spread far and wide, and vast numbers of people came to see him. Jesus instructed his disciples to have a boat ready so the crowd would not crush him. He had healed many people that day, so all the sick people eagerly pushed forward to touch him" (Mark 3:8-10 NLT).

147. POWER TO HEAL SICKNESSES

"Then He appointed twelve, that they might be with Him and that He might send them out to preach, and to have power to heal sicknesses and to cast out demons" (Mark 3:15 NKJV).

148. TWO ACCOUNTS OF HEALING

"Then a leader of the local synagogue, whose name was Jairus, arrived. When he saw Jesus, he fell at his feet, pleading fervently with him. 'My little daughter is dying,' he said. 'Please come and lay your hands on her; heal her so she can live.' Jesus went with him, and all the people followed, crowding around him. A woman in the crowd had suffered for twelve years with constant bleeding. She had suffered a great deal from many doctors, and over the years she had spent everything she had to pay them, but she had gotten no better. In fact, she had gotten worse. She had heard about Jesus, so she came up behind him through the crowd and touched his robe. For she thought to herself, 'If I can just touch his robe, I will be healed.' Immediately the bleeding stopped, and she could feel in her body that she had been healed of her terrible condition. Jesus realized at once that healing power had gone out from him, so he turned around in the crowd and asked, 'Who touched my robe?' His disciples said to him, 'Look at this crowd pressing around you. How can you ask, 'Who touched me?"' But he kept on looking around to see who had done it. Then the frightened woman, trembling at the realization of what had happened to her, came and fell to her knees in front of him and told him what she had done. And he said to her, 'Daughter, your faith has made you well. Go in peace. Your suffering is over.' While he was still speaking to her, messengers arrived from the home of Jairus, the leader of the synagogue. They told him, 'Your daughter is dead. There's no use troubling the Teacher now.' But Jesus overheard them and said to Jairus, 'Don't be afraid. Just have faith.' Then Jesus stopped the crowd and wouldn't let anyone go with him except Peter, James, and John (the brother of James). When they came to the home of the synagogue leader, Jesus saw much commotion and weeping and wailing. He went inside and asked, 'Why all this commotion and weeping? The child isn't dead; she's only asleep.' The crowd laughed at him. But he made them all leave, and he took the girl's father and mother and his three disciples into the room where the girl was lying. Holding her hand, he said to her, 'Talitha koum,' which means 'Little girl, get up!' And the girl, who was twelve years old, immediately stood up and walked around! They were overwhelmed and totally amazed" (Mark 5:22-42 NLT).

149. THE DISCIPLES ANOINT THE SICK

"Calling the Twelve to him, he sent them out two by two and gave them authority over evil spirits ... They went out and preached that people should repent. They drove out many demons and anointed many sick people with oil and healed them" (Mark 6:7, 12-13 NIV).

150. TOUCHING THE HEM OF JESUS' GARMENT

"They ran throughout that whole region and carried the sick on mats to wherever they heard he was. And wherever he went—into villages, towns or countryside—they placed the sick in the marketplaces. They begged him to let them touch even the edge of his cloak, and all who touched it were healed" (Mark 6:55-56 NIV).

151. OPENING A DEAF MAN'S EARS

"Jesus left Tyre and went up to Sidon before going back to the Sea of Galilee and the region of the Ten Towns. A deaf man with a speech impediment was brought to him, and the people begged Jesus to lay his hands on the man to heal him. Jesus led him away from the crowd so they could be alone. He put his fingers into the man's ears. Then, spitting on his own fingers, he touched the man's tongue. Looking up to heaven, he sighed and said, 'Ephphatha,' which means, 'Be opened!' Instantly the man could hear perfectly, and his tongue was freed so he could speak plainly! Jesus told the crowd not to tell anyone, but the more he told them not to, the more they spread the news. They were completely amazed and said again and again, 'Everything he does is wonderful. He even makes the deaf to hear and gives speech to those who cannot speak'" (Mark 7:31-37 NLT).

152. JESUS HEALS A BLIND MAN

"When they arrived at Bethsaida, some people brought a blind man to Jesus, and they begged him to touch the man and heal him. Jesus took the blind man by the hand and led him out of the village. Then, spitting on the man's eyes, he laid his hands on him and asked, 'Can you see anything now?' The man looked around. 'Yes,' he said, 'I see people, but I can't see them very clearly. They look like trees walking around.' Then Jesus placed his hands on the man's eyes again, and his eyes were opened. His sight was completely restored, and he could see everything clearly" (Mark 8:22-25 NLT).

153. ANYTHING IS POSSIBLE FOR THOSE WHO BELIEVE

"One of the men in the crowd spoke up and said, 'Teacher, I brought my son so you could heal him. He is possessed by an evil spirit that won't let him talk. And whenever this spirit seizes him, it throws him violently to the ground. Then he foams at the mouth and grinds his teeth and becomes rigid. So I asked your disciples to cast out the evil spirit, but they couldn't do it.' Jesus said to them, 'You faithless people! How long must I be with you? How long must I put up with you? Bring the boy to me.' So they brought the boy. But when the evil spirit saw Jesus, it threw the child into a violent convulsion, and he fell to the ground, writhing and foaming at the mouth. 'How long has this been happening?' Jesus asked the boy's father. He replied, 'Since he was a little boy. The spirit often throws him into the fire or into water, trying to kill him. Have mercy on us and help us, if you can.' 'What do you mean, 'If I can'?' Jesus asked, 'Anything is possible if a person believes.' The father instantly cried out, "I do believe, but help me overcome my unbelief!" When Jesus saw that the crowd of onlookers was growing, he rebuked the evil spirit. 'Listen, you spirit that makes this boy unable to hear and speak,' he said. 'I command you to come out of this child and never enter him again!' Then the spirit screamed and threw the boy into another violent convulsion and left him. The boy appeared to be dead. A murmur ran through the crowd as people said, 'He's dead.' But Jesus took him by the hand and helped him to his feet, and he stood up" (Mark 9:17-26 NLT).

154. WITH GOD ALL THINGS ARE POSSIBLE

"Jesus looked at them and said, 'With man this is impossible, but not with God; all things are possible with God'" (Mark 10:27 NIV).

155. BLIND BARTIMAEUS' HEALING

"Then they reached Jericho, and as Jesus and his disciples left town, a large crowd followed him. A blind beggar named Bartimaeus (son of Timaeus) was sitting beside the road. When Bartimaeus heard that Jesus of Nazareth was nearby, he began to shout, 'Jesus, Son of David, have mercy on me!' 'Be quiet!' many of the people yelled at him. But he only shouted louder, 'Son of David, have mercy on me!' When Jesus heard him, he stopped and said, 'Tell him to come here.' So they called the blind man. 'Cheer up,' they said. 'Come on, he's calling you!' Bartimaeus threw aside his coat, jumped up, and came to Jesus. 'What do you want me to do for you?' Jesus asked. 'My Rabbi,' the blind man said, 'I want to see!' And Jesus said to him, 'Go, for your faith has healed you.' Instantly the man could see, and he followed Jesus down the road" (Mark 10:46-52 NLT).

156. YOU CAN PRAY FOR ANYTHING

"I tell you, you can pray for anything, and if you believe that you've received it, it will be yours" (Mark 11:24 NLT).

157. SIGNS ACCOMPANY THOSE WHO BELIEVE

"Jesus said to them, 'Go into all the world and preach the gospel to all creation. Whoever believes and is baptized will be saved, but whoever does not believe will be condemned. And these signs will accompany those who believe: In my name they will drive out demons; they will speak in new tongues; they will pick up snakes with their hands; and when they drink deadly poison, it will not hurt them at all; they will place their hands on sick people, and they will get well'" (Mark 16:15-20 NIV).

158. NOTHING IS IMPOSSIBLE

"For nothing is impossible with God" (Luke 1:37 NLT).

159. RECOVERY OF SIGHT

"He went to Nazareth, where he had been brought up, and on the Sabbath day he went into the synagogue, as was his custom. And he stood up to read. The scroll of the prophet Isaiah was handed to him. Unrolling it, he found the place where it is written: 'The Spirit of the Lord is on me, because he has anointed me to preach good news to the poor. He has sent me to proclaim freedom for the prisoners and recovery of sight for the blind, to release the oppressed, to proclaim the year of the Lord's favor.' Then he rolled up the scroll, gave it back to the attendant and sat down. The eyes of everyone in the synagogue were fastened on him, and he began by saying to them, 'Today this scripture is fulfilled in your hearing'" (Luke 4:16-21 NIV).

160. PETER'S MOTHER-IN-LAW RESTORED

"Jesus left the synagogue and went to the home of Simon. Now Simon's mother-in-law was suffering from a high fever, and they asked Jesus to help her. So he bent over her and rebuked the fever, and it left her. She got up at once and began to wait on them" (Luke 4:38-39 NIV).

161. THE TOUCH OF HIS HAND

"As the sun went down that evening, people throughout the village brought sick family members to Jesus. No matter what their diseases were, the touch of his hand healed every one" (Luke 4:40 NLT).

162. JESUS IS WILLING TO HEAL

"In one of the villages, Jesus met a man with an advanced case of leprosy. When the man saw Jesus, he bowed with his face to the ground, begging to be healed. 'Lord,' he said, 'if you are willing, you can heal me and make me clean.' Jesus reached out and touched him. 'I am willing,' he said. 'Be healed!' And instantly the leprosy disappeared. Then Jesus instructed him not to tell anyone what had happened. He said, 'Go to the priest and let him examine you. Take along the offering required in the law of Moses for those who have been healed of leprosy. This will be a public testimony that you have been cleansed.' But despite Jesus' instructions, the report of his power spread even faster, and vast crowds came to hear him preach and to be healed of their diseases. But Jesus often withdrew to the wilderness for prayer" (Luke 5:12-16 NLT).

163. THE POWER OF THE LORD WAS PRESENT TO HEAL

"One day, as Jesus was teaching, some Pharisees and teachers of the Law happened to be sitting nearby. The people had come from every village in Galilee and Judea and from Jerusalem. The power of the Lord was present to heal them" (Luke 5:17 ISV).

164. WONDER AND AWE

"Some men came carrying a paralyzed man on a sleeping mat. They tried to take him inside to Jesus, but they couldn't reach him because of the crowd. So they went up to the roof and took off some tiles. Then they lowered the sick man on his mat down into the crowd, right in front of Jesus. Seeing their faith, Jesus said to the man, 'Young man, your sins are forgiven.' But the Pharisees and teachers of religious law said to themselves, 'Who does he think he is? That's blasphemy! Only God can forgive sins!' Jesus knew what they were thinking, so he asked them, 'Why do you question this in your hearts? Is it easier to say 'Your sins are forgiven,' or 'Stand up and walk'? So I will prove to you that the Son of Man has the authority on earth to forgive sins.' Then Jesus turned to the paralyzed man and said, 'Stand up, pick up your mat, and go home!' And immediately, as everyone watched, the man jumped up, picked up his mat, and went home praising God. Everyone was gripped with great wonder and awe, and they praised God, exclaiming, 'We have seen amazing things today!'" (Luke 5:18-26 NLT).

165. HEALING ON THE SABBATH

"And it came to pass also on another Sabbath, that he entered into the synagogue and taught: and there was a man whose right hand was withered. And the scribes and Pharisees watched him, whether he would heal on the Sabbath day; that they might find an accusation against him. But he knew their thoughts, and said to the man which had the withered hand, 'Rise up, and stand forth in the midst.' And he arose and stood forth. Then said Jesus unto them, 'I will ask you one thing; Is it lawful on the Sabbath days to do good, or to do evil? to save life, or to destroy it?' And looking round about upon them all, he said unto the man, 'Stretch forth thy hand.' And he did so: and his hand was restored whole as the other" (Luke 6:6-10 NKJV).

166. POWER EMANATED FROM JESUS

"He went down with them and stood on a level place. A large crowd of his disciples was there and a great number of people from all over Judea, from Jerusalem, and from the coastal region around Tyre and Sidon, who had come to hear him and to be healed of their diseases. Those troubled by impure spirits were cured, and the people all tried to touch him, because power was coming from him and healing them all" (Luke 6:17-19 NIV).

167. THE HEALING OF ROMAN OFFICER'S SERVANT

"When Jesus had finished saying all this to the people, he returned to Capernaum. At that time the highly valued slave of a Roman officer was sick and near death. When the officer heard about Jesus, he sent some respected Jewish elders to ask him to come and heal his slave. So they earnestly begged Jesus to help the man. 'If anyone deserves your help, he does,' they said, 'for he loves the Jewish people and even built a synagogue for us.' So Jesus went with them. But just before they arrived at the house, the officer sent some friends to say, 'Lord, don't trouble yourself by coming to my home, for I am not worthy of such an honor. I am not even worthy to come and meet you. Just say the word from where you are, and my servant will be healed. I know this because I am under the authority of my superior officers, and I have authority over my soldiers. I only need to say, 'Go,' and they go, or 'Come,' and they come. And if I say to my slaves, 'Do this,' they do it.' When Jesus heard this, he was amazed. Turning to the crowd that was following him, he said, 'I tell you, I haven't seen faith like this in all Israel!' And when the officer's friends returned to his house, they found the slave completely healed" (Luke 7:1-10 NLT).

168. A YOUNG MAN RESUSCITATED

"Soon afterward Jesus went with his disciples to the village of Nain, and a large crowd followed him. A funeral procession was coming out as he approached the village gate. The young man who had died was a widow's only son, and a large crowd from the village was with her. When the Lord saw her, his heart overflowed with compassion. 'Don't cry!' he said. Then he walked over to the coffin and touched it, and the bearers stopped. 'Young man,' he said, 'I tell you, get up.' Then the dead boy sat up and began to talk! And Jesus gave him back to his mother" (Luke 7:11-17 NLT).

169. THE BLIND SEE, THE LAME WALK, AND THE DEAF HEAR

"The disciples of John the Baptist told John about everything Jesus was doing. So John called for two of his disciples, and he sent them to the Lord to ask him, 'Are you the Messiah we've been expecting, or should we keep looking for someone else?' John's two disciples found Jesus and said to him, 'John the Baptist sent us to ask, 'Are you the Messiah we've been expecting, or should we keep looking for someone else?' At that very time, Jesus cured many people of their diseases, illnesses, and evil spirits, and he restored sight to many who were blind. Then he told John's disciples, 'Go back to John and tell him what you have seen and heard—the blind see, the lame walk, those with leprosy are cured, the deaf hear, the dead are raised to life, and the Good News is being preached to the poor.' And he added, 'God blesses those who do not fall away because of me'" (Luke 7:18-23 NLT).

170. WOMEN CURED OF DISEASES

"Soon afterward Jesus began a tour of the nearby towns and villages, preaching and announcing the Good News about the Kingdom of God. He took his twelve disciples with him, along with some women who had been cured of evil spirits and diseases" (Luke 8:1-2 NLT).

171. HEALING THE OPPRESSED

"Then those who had seen what happened told the others how the demon-possessed man had been healed" (Luke 8:36 NLT).

172. YOUR FAITH HAS HEALED YOU

"As Jesus was on his way, the crowds almost crushed him. And a woman was there who had been subject to bleeding for twelve years, but no one could heal her. She came up behind him and touched the edge of his cloak, and immediately her bleeding stopped. 'Who touched me?' Jesus asked. When they all denied it, Peter said, 'Master, the people are crowding and pressing against you.' But Jesus said, 'Someone touched me; I know that power has gone out from me.' Then the woman, seeing that she could not go unnoticed, came trembling and fell at his feet. In the presence of all the people, she told why she had touched him and how she had been instantly healed. Then he said to her, 'Daughter, your faith has healed you. Go in peace'" (Luke 8:42-48 NIV).

173. JUST BELIEVE

"While Jesus was still speaking, someone came from the house of Jairus, the synagogue leader. 'Your daughter is dead,' he said. 'Don't bother the teacher anymore.' Hearing this, Jesus said to Jairus, 'Don't be afraid; just believe, and she will be healed.' When he arrived at the house of Jairus, he did not let anyone go in with him except Peter, John and James, and the child's father and mother. Meanwhile, all the people were wailing and mourning for her. 'Stop wailing,' Jesus said. 'She is not dead but asleep.' They laughed at him, knowing that she was dead. He took her by the hand and said, 'My child, get up!' Her spirit returned, and at once she stood up. Then Jesus told them to give her something to eat. Her parents were astonished, but he ordered them not to tell anyone what had happened" (Luke 8:49-56 NIV).

174. AUTHORITY TO HEAL

"One day Jesus called together his twelve disciples and gave them power and authority to cast out all demons and to heal all diseases. Then he sent them out to tell everyone about the Kingdom of God and to heal the sick. 'Take nothing for your journey,' he instructed them. 'Don't take a walking stick, a traveler's bag, food, money, or even a change of clothes. Wherever you go, stay in the same house until you leave town. And if a town refuses to welcome you, shake its dust from your feet as you leave to show that you have abandoned those people to their fate.' So they began their circuit of the villages, preaching the Good News and healing the sick" (Luke 9:1-6 NLT).

175. HEALING THE SICK

"The crowds found out where he was going, and they followed him. He welcomed them and taught them about the Kingdom of God, and he healed those who were sick" (Luke 9:11 NLT).

176. A MAJESTIC DISPLAY OF GOD'S POWER

"The next day, after they had come down the mountain, a large crowd met Jesus. A man in the crowd called out to him, 'Teacher, I beg you to look at my son, my only child. An evil spirit keeps seizing him, making him scream. It throws him into convulsions so that he foams at the mouth. It batters him and hardly ever leaves him alone. I begged your disciples to cast out the spirit, but they couldn't do it.' Jesus said, 'You faithless and corrupt people! How long must I be with you and put up with you?' Then he said to the man, 'Bring your son here.' As the boy came forward, the demon knocked him to the ground and threw him into a violent convulsion. But Jesus rebuked the evil spirit and healed the boy. Then he gave him back to his father. Awe gripped the people as they saw this majestic display of God's power" (Luke 9:37-43 NLT).

177. JESUS DOESN'T DESTROY LIVES

"The Son of Man did not come to destroy men's lives, but to save them" (Luke 8:56 NASB).

178. HEAL THE SICK AND RELEASE THE KINGDOM

"After these things the Lord appointed seventy others also, and sent them two by two before His face into every city and place where He Himself was about to go. Then He said to them … 'heal the sick who are there, and say to them, 'The kingdom of God has come near to you … Behold, I give you the authority to trample on serpents and scorpions, and over all the power of the enemy, and nothing shall by any means hurt you'" (Luke 10:1-2, 9, 19 NKJV).

179. WHEN JESUS TOUCHED HER, SHE STOOD STRAIGHT

"One Sabbath day as Jesus was teaching in a synagogue, he saw a woman who had been crippled by an evil spirit. She had been bent double for eighteen years and was unable to stand up straight. When Jesus saw her, he called her over and said, 'Dear woman, you are healed of your sickness!' Then he touched her, and instantly she could stand straight. How she praised God!" (Luke 13:10-13 BSB).

180. JESUS' PURPOSE

"I will keep on casting out demons and healing people today and tomorrow; and the third day I will accomplish my purpose" (Luke 13:32b NLT).

181. WHAT IS THE SABBATH FOR?

"One Sabbath day Jesus went to eat dinner in the home of a leader of the Pharisees, and the people were watching him closely. There was a man there whose arms and legs were swollen. Jesus asked the Pharisees and experts in religious law, 'Is it permitted in the law to heal people on the Sabbath day, or not?' When they refused to answer, Jesus touched the sick man and healed him and sent him away. Then he turned to them and said, 'Which of you doesn't work on the Sabbath? If your son or your cow falls into a pit, don't you rush to get him out?'" (Luke 14:1-5 NLT).

182. THANKFULNESS RELEASES HEALING

"As Jesus continued on toward Jerusalem, he reached the border between Galilee and Samaria. As he entered a village there, ten men with leprosy stood at a distance, crying out, 'Jesus, Master, have mercy on us!' He looked at them and said, 'Go show yourselves to the priests.' And as they went, they were cleansed of their leprosy. One of them, when he saw that he was healed, came back to Jesus, shouting, 'Praise God!' He fell to the ground at Jesus' feet, thanking him for what he had done. This man was a Samaritan. Jesus asked, 'Didn't I heal ten men? Where are the other nine? Has no one returned to give glory to God except this foreigner?' And Jesus said to the man, 'Stand up and go. Your faith has healed you'" (Luke 17:11-17 NLT).

183. GOD DOES THE IMPOSSIBLE

"He said, 'The things that are impossible with people are possible with God'" (Luke 18:27 NASB).

184. WHAT DO YOU WANT?

"As Jesus approached Jericho, a blind beggar was sitting beside the road. When he heard the noise of a crowd going past, he asked what was happening. They told him that Jesus the Nazarene was going by. So he began shouting, 'Jesus, Son of David, have mercy on me!' 'Be quiet!' the people in front yelled at him. But he only shouted louder, 'Son of David, have mercy on me!' When Jesus heard him, he stopped and ordered that the man be brought to him. As the man came near, Jesus asked him, 'What do you want me to do for you?' 'Lord,' he said, 'I want to see!' And Jesus said, 'All right, receive your sight! Your faith has healed you.' Instantly the man could see, and he followed Jesus, praising God. And all who saw it praised God, too" (Luke 18:35-43 NLT).

185. HEALING A SEVERED EAR

"One of them struck at the high priest's slave, slashing off his right ear. But Jesus said, 'No more of this.' And he touched the man's ear and healed him" (Luke 22:50-51 NET).

186. JESUS IS LIFE

"In him was life, and that life was the light of all mankind" (John 1:4).

187. SIGNS AND WONDERS STIR BELIEF

"As he traveled through Galilee, he came to Cana, where he had turned the water into wine. There was a government official in nearby Capernaum whose son was very sick. When he heard that Jesus had come from Judea to Galilee, he went and begged Jesus to come to Capernaum to heal his son, who was about to die. Jesus asked, 'Will you never believe in me unless you see miraculous signs and wonders?' The official pleaded, 'Lord, please come now before my little boy dies.' Then Jesus told him, 'Go back home. Your son will live!' And the man believed what Jesus said and started home. While the man was on his way, some of his servants met him with the news that his son was alive and well. He asked them when the boy had begun to get better, and they replied, 'Yesterday afternoon at one o'clock his fever suddenly disappeared!' Then the father realized that that was the very time Jesus had told him, 'Your son will live.' And he and his entire household believed in Jesus" (John 4:46-53 NLT).

188. HEALING AT THE POOL OF BETHESDA

"Some time later, Jesus went up to Jerusalem for one of the Jewish festivals. Now there is in Jerusalem near the Sheep Gate a pool, which in Aramaic is called Bethesda and which is surrounded by five covered colonnades. Here a great number of disabled people used to lie—the blind, the lame, the paralyzed. One who was there had been an invalid for thirty-eight years. When Jesus saw him lying there and learned that he had been in this condition for a long time, he asked him, 'Do you want to get well?' 'Sir,' the invalid replied, 'I have no one to help me into the pool when the water is stirred. While I am trying to get in, someone else goes down ahead of me.' Then Jesus said to him, 'Get up! Pick up your mat and walk.' At once the man was cured; he picked up his mat and walked. The day on which this took place was a Sabbath, and so the Jews said to the man who had been healed, 'It is the Sabbath; the law forbids you to carry your mat.' But he replied, 'The man who made me well said to me, 'Pick up your mat and walk.'' So they asked him, 'Who is this fellow who told you to pick it up and walk?' The man who was healed had no idea who it was, for Jesus had slipped away into the crowd that was there. Later Jesus found him at the temple and said to him, 'See, you are well again. Stop sinning or something worse may happen to you.'" (John 5:1-14 NIV).

189. JESUS HEALS A BLIND MAN

"As Jesus was walking along, he saw a man who had been blind from birth. 'Rabbi,' his disciples asked him, 'Why was this man born blind? Was it because of his own sins or his parents' sins?' 'It was not because of his sins or his parents' sins,' Jesus answered. 'This happened so the power of God could be seen in him. We must quickly carry out the tasks assigned us by the one who sent us. The night is coming, and then no one can work. But while I am here in the world, I am the light of the world.' Then he spit on the ground, made mud with the saliva, and spread the mud over the blind man's eyes. He told him, 'Go wash yourself in the pool of Siloam' (Siloam means "sent"). So the man went and washed and came back seeing!" (John 9:1-7 NLT).

190. THAT YOU MAY HAVE LIFE

"The thief comes only to steal and kill and destroy; I have come that they may have life, and have it to the full" (John 10:10 NIV).

191. JESUS PERFORMS MIRACULOUS SIGNS

"Some went to the Pharisees and told them what Jesus had done. Then the leading priests and Pharisees called the high council together. 'What are we going to do?' they asked each other. 'This man certainly performs many miraculous signs. If we allow him to go on like this, soon everyone will believe in him'" (John 11:46-48 NLT).

192. MIRACULOUS SIGNS INSPIRE BELIEF

"Believe me that I am in the Father, and the Father is in me, but if you do not believe me, believe because of the miraculous deeds themselves" (John 14:11 ESV).

193. HEALINGS ABOUNDED IN JESUS' MINISTRY

"The disciples saw Jesus do many other miraculous signs in addition to the ones recorded in this book" (John 20:30 NLT).

194. JESUS' UNRECORDED HEALINGS

"Jesus also did many other things. If they were all written down, I suppose the whole world could not contain the books that would be written" (John 21:25 NLT).

195. WONDERS AND MIRACULOUS SIGNS

"Men of Israel, listen to these words: Jesus the Nazarene, a man clearly attested to you by God with powerful deeds, wonders, and miraculous signs that God performed among you through him, just as you yourselves know" (Acts 2:22 ESV).

196. HEALED AT THE BEAUTIFUL GATE

"Peter and John went to the Temple one afternoon to take part in the three o'clock prayer service. As they approached the Temple, a man lame from birth was being carried in. Each day he was put beside the Temple gate, the one called the Beautiful Gate, so he could beg from the people going into the Temple. When he saw Peter and John about to enter, he asked them for some money. Peter and John looked at him intently, and Peter said, 'Look at us!' The lame man looked at them eagerly, expecting some money. But Peter said, 'I don't have any silver or gold for you. But I'll give you what I have. In the name of Jesus Christ the Nazarene, get up and walk!' Then Peter took the lame man by the right hand and helped him up. And as he did, the man's feet and ankles were instantly healed and strengthened. He jumped up, stood on his feet, and began to walk! Then, walking, leaping, and praising God, he went into the Temple with them" (Acts 3:1-8 NLT).

197. HEALED IN JESUS' NAME

"By faith in the name of Jesus, this man whom you see and know was made strong. It is Jesus' name and the faith that comes through him that has completely healed him, as you can all see" (Acts 3:16 NIV).

198. STRETCH OUT YOUR HAND

"And now, O Lord, hear their threats, and give us, your servants, great boldness in preaching your word. Stretch out your hand with healing power; may miraculous signs and wonders be done through the name of your holy servant Jesus" (Acts 4:29-30 NLT).

199. HEALED BY PETER'S SHADOW

"The apostles were performing many miraculous signs and wonders among the people. And all the believers were meeting regularly at the Temple in the area known as Solomon's Colonnade. But no one else dared to join them, even though all the people had high regard for them. Yet more and more people believed and were brought to the Lord—crowds of both men and women. As a result of the apostles' work, sick people were brought out into the streets on beds and mats so that Peter's shadow might fall across some of them as he went by" (Acts 5:12-15 NLT).

200. CROWDS ARE HEALED

"Crowds came from the villages around Jerusalem, bringing their sick and those possessed by evil spirits, and they were all healed" (Acts 5:16 NLT).

201. HEALING IS AN OUTWORKING OF GRACE

"Now Stephen, a man full of God's grace and power, did great wonders and miraculous signs among the people" (Acts 6:8 NIV).

202. PARALYTICS AND CRIPPLES HEALED

"Philip went down to a city in Samaria and proclaimed the Christ there. When the crowds heard Philip and saw the miraculous signs he did, they all paid close attention to what he said. With shrieks, evil spirits came out of many, and many paralytics and cripples were healed" (Acts 8:5-7 NIV).

203. SAUL REGAINS SIGHT

Ananias went and found Saul. He laid his hands on him and said, 'Brother Saul, the Lord Jesus, who appeared to you on the road, has sent me so that you might regain your sight and be filled with the Holy Spirit.' Instantly something like scales fell from Saul's eyes, and he regained his sight. Then he got up and was baptized" (Acts 9:17-18 NLT).

204. JESUS CHRIST HEALS YOU

"There he found a man named Aeneas, who was paralyzed and had been bedridden for eight years. 'Aeneas,' Peter said to him, 'Jesus Christ heals you. Get up and roll up your mat.' Immediately Aeneas got up. All those who lived in Lydda and Sharon saw him and turned to the Lord" (Acts 9:33-35 NIV).

205. A WOMAN'S RESUSCITATION

"In Joppa there was a disciple named Tabitha (in Greek her name is Dorcas); she was always doing good and helping the poor. About that time she became sick and died, and her body was washed and placed in an upstairs room. Lydda was near Joppa; so when the disciples heard that Peter was in Lydda, they sent two men to him and urged him, 'Please come at once!' Peter went with them, and when he arrived he was taken upstairs to the room. All the widows stood around him, crying and showing him the robes and other clothing that Dorcas had made while she was still with them. Peter sent them all out of the room; then he got down on his knees and prayed. Turning toward the dead woman, he said, 'Tabitha, get up.' She opened her eyes, and seeing Peter she sat up. He took her by the hand and helped her to her feet. Then he called for the believers, especially the widows, and presented her to them alive. This became known all over Joppa, and many people believed in the Lord" (Acts 9:36-42 NIV).

206. HEALING IS GOOD

"How God anointed Jesus of Nazareth with the Holy Spirit and power, and how he went around doing good and healing all who were under the power of the devil, because God was with him" (Acts 10:38 NIV).

207. A LAME MAN HEALED

"In Lystra there sat a man who was lame. He had been that way from birth and had never walked. He listened to Paul as he was speaking. Paul looked directly at him, saw that he had faith to be healed and called out, 'Stand up on your feet!' At that, the man jumped up and began to walk" (Acts 14:8-10 NIV).

208. HEALING THROUGH HANDKERCHIEFS

"God did extraordinary miracles through Paul, so that even handkerchiefs and aprons that had touched him were taken to the sick, and their illnesses were cured and the evil spirits left them" (Acts 19:11-12 NIV).

209. EUTYCHUS' RESUSCITATION

"As Paul spoke on and on, a young man named Eutychus, sitting on the windowsill, became very drowsy. Finally, he fell sound asleep and dropped three stories to his death below. Paul went down, bent over him, and took him into his arms. 'Don't worry,' he said, 'he's alive!' Then they all went back upstairs, shared in the Lord's Supper, and ate together. Paul continued talking to them until dawn, and then he left" (Acts 20:9-11 NLT).

210. EYESIGHT REGAINED

"I was blinded by the intense light and had to be led by the hand to Damascus by my companions. A man named Ananias lived there. He was a godly man, deeply devoted to the law, and well regarded by all the Jews of Damascus. He came and stood beside me and said, 'Brother Saul, regain your sight.' And that very moment I could see him!" (Acts 22:11-13 NLT).

211. STOPPING THE EFFECTS OF A SNAKEBITE

"As Paul gathered an armful of sticks and was laying them on the fire, a poisonous snake, driven out by the heat, bit him on the hand. The people of the island saw it hanging from his hand and said to each other, 'A murderer, no doubt! Though he escaped the sea, justice will not permit him to live.' But Paul shook off the snake into the fire and was unharmed. The people waited for him to swell up or suddenly drop dead. But when they had waited a long time and saw that he wasn't harmed, they changed their minds"(Acts 28:3-6a NLT).

212. FEVER AND DYSENTERY HEALED

"Near the shore where we landed was an estate belonging to Publius, the chief official of the island. He welcomed us and treated us kindly for three days. As it happened, Publius's father was ill with fever and dysentery. Paul went in and prayed for him, and laying his hands on him, he healed him. Then all the other sick people on the island came and were healed. As a result we were showered with honors, and when the time came to sail, people supplied us with everything we would need for the trip" (Acts 28:7-10 NLT).

213. A HARD-HEART IS AN OBSTACLE TO HEALING

"For the hearts of these people are hardened, and their ears cannot hear, and they have closed their eyes—so their eyes cannot see, and their ears cannot hear, and their hearts cannot understand, and they cannot turn to me and let me heal them" (Acts 28:27 NLT).

214. THE SPIRIT ENLIVENS OUR BODIES

"The Spirit of God, who raised Jesus from the dead, lives in you. And just as God raised Christ Jesus from the dead, he will give life to your mortal bodies by this same Spirit living within you" (Romans 8:11 NLT).

215. UNTO SAVING HEALTH

"For with the heart one believes unto righteousness, and with the mouth confession is made unto saving health" (Romans 10:10 JUB).

216. FULLY PROCLAIMING THE GOSPEL

"I will not venture to speak of anything except what Christ has accomplished through me in leading the Gentiles to obey God by what I have said and done—by the power of signs and wonders, through the power of the Spirit of God. So from Jerusalem all the way around to Illyricum, I have fully proclaimed the gospel of Christ" (Romans 15:18-19 NIV).

217. A DEMONSTRATION OF THE SPIRIT

"For I resolved to know nothing while I was with you except Jesus Christ and him crucified. I came to you in weakness with great fear and trembling. My message and my preaching were not with wise and persuasive words, but with a demonstration of the Spirit's power, so that your faith might not rest on human wisdom, but on God's power" (1 Corinthians 2:2-5 NIV).

218. DISCERNING THE BODY

"Therefore, whoever eats the bread or drinks the cup of the Lord in an unworthy manner will be guilty of sinning against the body and blood of the Lord. A man ought to examine himself before he eats of the bread and drinks of the cup. For anyone who eats and drinks without recognizing the body of the Lord eats and drinks judgment on himself. That is why many among you are weak and sick, and a number of you have fallen asleep" (1 Corinthians 11:27-30 BSB).

219. HEALING GRACE

"A spiritual gift is given to each of us so we can help each other. To one person the Spirit gives ... the gift of healing" (1 Corinthians 12:7-8a, 9 NLT).

220. GIFTS OF HEALING

"God has appointed in the church first apostles, second prophets, third teachers, then miracles, then gifts of healing, helping, administrating, and various kinds of tongues" (1 Corinthians 12:28 ESV).

221. DELIVERED FROM DEADLY PERIL

"God has delivered us from such a deadly peril, and he will deliver us again. On him we have set our hope that he will continue to deliver us" (2 Corinthians 1:10 NIV).

222. THE LIFE OF JESUS CAN BE REVEALED IN THE BODY

"We always carry around in our body the death of Jesus, so that the life of Jesus may also be revealed in our body" (2 Corinthians 4:10 NIV).

223. THE DAY OF SALVATION

"For he says, 'In the time of my favor I heard you, and in the day of salvation [deliverance, healing] I helped you.' I tell you, now is the time of God's favor, now is the day of salvation [deliverance, healing]" (2 Corinthians 6:2 NIV).

224. JESUS REDEEMED US FROM THE CURSE OF SICKNESS

"Christ has rescued us from the curse pronounced by the law. When he was hung on the cross, he took upon himself the curse for our wrongdoing. For it is written in the Scriptures, 'Cursed is everyone who is hung on a tree'" (Galatians 3:13 NLT).

225. ALL THINGS ARE UNDER THE FEET OF JESUS

"God has put all things under the authority of Christ and has made him head over all things for the benefit of the church" (Ephesians 1:22 NLT).

226. HEALING IS AN EXPRESSION OF GOD'S MERCY

"I thought I should send Epaphroditus back to you. He is a true brother, co-worker, and fellow soldier. And he was your messenger to help me in my need. For he longs for all of you and is distressed because you heard he was ill. Indeed he was ill, and almost died. But God had mercy on him, and not on him only but also on me, to spare me sorrow upon sorrow" (Philippians 2:25-27 NLT).

227. RESCUED FROM THE IMPACT OF SATAN'S KINGDOM

"God has rescued us from the dominion of darkness and brought us into the kingdom of the Son he loves" (Colossians 1:13 NIV).

228. THE PRESERVATION OF THE BODY

"Now may the God of peace Himself sanctify you entirely; and may your spirit and soul and body be preserved complete, without blame at the coming of our Lord Jesus Christ" (1 Thessalonians 5:23 NLT).

229. DELIVERED FROM EVERY EVIL ATTACK

"The Lord will deliver me from every evil attack and will bring me safely into his heavenly Kingdom. All glory to God forever and ever! Amen" (2 Timothy 4:18 NLT).

230. HEALING, A DISPLAY OF GOD'S GRACE

"For the grace of God has displayed itself with healing power to all mankind" (Titus 2:11 WNT).

231. EVERY BLESSING IS OURS IN MESSIAH

"I pray that your partnership in the faith may become effective as you fully acknowledge every blessing that is ours in the Messiah" (Philemon 1:6 ISV).

232. HEALING TESTIFIES TO SALVATION

"How shall we escape if we ignore such a great salvation? This salvation, which was first announced by the Lord, was confirmed to us by those who heard him. God also testified to it by signs, wonders and various miracles, and gifts of the Holy Spirit distributed according to his will" (Hebrews 2:3-4 NIV).

233. STRENGTHEN WEAK HANDS AND FEEBLE FEET

"Strengthen the hands that are weak and the knees that are feeble, and make straight paths for your feet, so that the limb which is lame may not be put out of joint, but rather be healed" (Hebrews 12:12-13 NIV).

234. JESUS STILL HEALS

"Jesus Christ, the same yesterday, today and forever" (Hebrews 13:8 NLT).

235. THE PRAYER OF FAITH

"Is anyone among you in trouble? Let them pray. Is anyone happy? Let them sing songs of praise. Is anyone among you sick? Let them call the elders of the church to pray over them and anoint them with oil in the name of the Lord. And the prayer offered in faith will make the sick person well; the Lord will raise them up. If they have sinned, they will be forgiven. Therefore confess your sins to each other and pray for each other so that you may be healed. The prayer of a righteous person is powerful and effective" (James 5:13-16 NIV).

236. BY HIS WOUNDS YOU'RE HEALED

"He personally carried our sins in his body on the cross so that we can be dead to sin and live for what is right. By his wounds you are healed" (1 Peter 2:24 NLT).

237. HIS DIVINE POWER HAS GRANTED US EVERYTHING

"His divine power has granted to us everything pertaining to life and godliness, through the true knowledge of Him who called us by His own glory and excellence" (2 Peter 1:3 NASB).

238. JESUS CAME TO DESTROY THE WORKS OF THE DEVIL

"For this purpose the Son of God was manifested, that He might destroy the works of the Devil" (1 John 3:8 NKJV).

239. PRAYER FOR GOOD HEALTH

"Dear friend, I pray that you may enjoy good health and that all may go well with you, even as your soul is getting along well" (3 John 2 NIV).

240. JESUS IS MAKING ALL THINGS NEW

"He will wipe away every tear from their eyes, and death shall be no more, neither shall there be mourning, nor crying, nor pain anymore, for the former things have passed away. And he who was seated on the throne said, 'Behold, I am making all things new'"(Revelation 21:4-5a ESV).

241. LEAVES OF HEALING

"On each side of the river stood the tree of life, bearing twelve crops of fruit, yielding its fruit every month. And the leaves of the tree are for the healing of the nations" (Revelation 22:2 NIV).

Also Available From Christos Publishing:

REGENERATION
A Complete History of Healing In the Christian Church

"This will surely become a foundational resource for anyone studying healing in the future."
—*Pneuma Journal*

"A comprehensive, if not groundbreaking, exploration of religious healing."
—*Kirkus Reviews*

Find out more at historyofhealing.org

Christos Publishing